Contents

World of piracy	4
Caribbean buccaneers	6
Dress like a pirate	8
Corsairs and privateers	10
Make a treasure chest	12
Pirate ships	14
Make a pirate flag	16
Life on board	18
Make a pirate's fruit salad	20
Attack at sea	22
Make a pirate's dagger	24
Treasure!	26
Make a treasure map and case	28
Timeline	30
Glossary	31
Index and Webfinder	32

World of piracy

Pirates are sea robbers who go in search of ships to raid and capture. They have been known and feared by sailors since ancient times. Although some pirates had an adventurous life, most were just cruel criminals, on the lookout for easy victims.

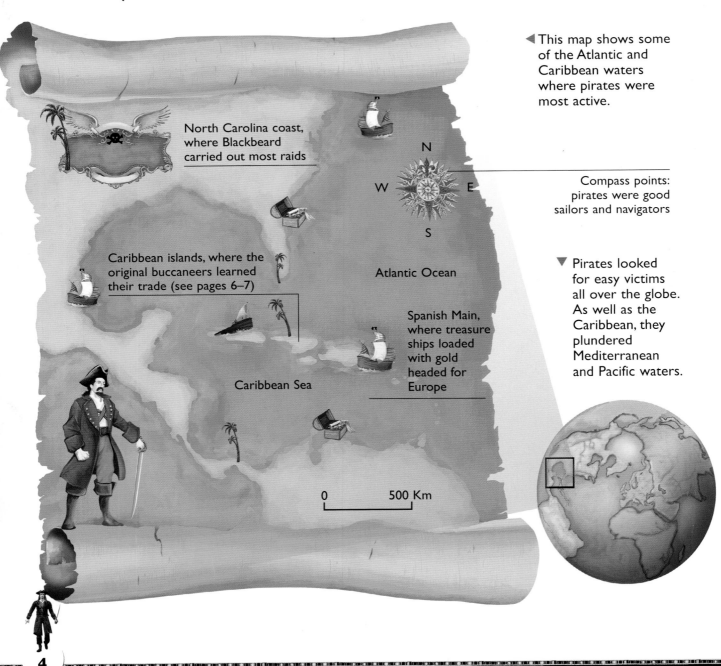

◄ This map shows some of the Atlantic and Caribbean waters where pirates were most active.

North Carolina coast, where Blackbeard carried out most raids

Compass points: pirates were good sailors and navigators

N
W   E
S

Caribbean islands, where the original buccaneers learned their trade (see pages 6–7)

Atlantic Ocean

Spanish Main, where treasure ships loaded with gold headed for Europe

Caribbean Sea

▼ Pirates looked for easy victims all over the globe. As well as the Caribbean, they plundered Mediterranean and Pacific waters.

0   500 Km

Robbery at sea

Piracy was a bloodthirsty business and was not for the faint-hearted. Some pirates would follow a treasure ship for days, waiting for the right moment to attack. Sometimes, they sailed into port and attacked coastal towns, too. They killed those who stood in their way and captured anyone who might be useful to them.

▼ Pirates were generally quick, strong and ferocious, which made them good fighters.

This famous pirate is called Blackbeard. He wielded a cutlass and had a number of pistols

Blackbeard

Edward Teach was one of the most famous and feared English pirates. He was also known as Blackbeard because of his long, dark beard. Though he spent most of his time at sea, Blackbeard was said to have 14 wives. He terrorized the eastern coast of America around the years 1717–18, stealing ships and capturing prisoners for ransom. This fearsome man finally died after a bloody battle with the British navy in America, when he slumped to the deck with 20 sword wounds and 5 bullet holes in his body. The lieutenant who killed him displayed Blackbeard's head from the ship's bowsprit.

Caribbean buccaneers

In the 17th century, Caribbean pirates were known as buccaneers. Their name comes from the French *boucan*, a grill used for cooking meat. The first buccaneers stole meat on the Caribbean islands to sell. They then began capturing ships at sea to steal treasures, too.

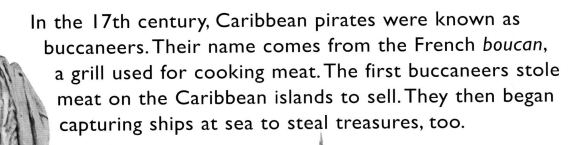

Weapons were brandished to threaten victims

◀ Morgan (in the hat, far left) attacked many cities along the coasts of Central and South America. He was ruthless in demanding that his victims give him all they possessed.

Jewels and valuables made up Morgan's favourite haul

This captive faces torture or death

Sir Henry Morgan

Henry Morgan was a famous Welsh buccaneer. He and his terrifying crew began raiding Spanish ships and colonies around the Caribbean Sea in the 1660s until his death in 1688. Morgan's achievements included destroying Panama City, the largest Spanish port in Central America. In 1674, Charles II, the King of England, knighted Morgan and made him deputy governor of Jamaica.

Hunting gear

Early buccaneers wore hunting gear. They had coarse shirts and tunics, with woollen breeches. They wrapped their head in a scarf, but always wore a hat if they could get hold of one.

Sword. Buccaneers were expert with muskets and knives, too

The cutlass was a deadly weapon

Mary Read was known as a good ▶ fighter, but the other pirates did not know she was a woman!

◀ Buccaneers were rough, tough men. Like all pirates, they took any opportunity to make money.

Women pirates

Piracy was a male business – or so men thought – and officially women were not allowed on board. But there were some famous female pirates. Anne Bonny was an Irish girl who dressed in men's clothes and sailed to the Bahamas with a pirate named Calico Jack Rackham. In 1719, Rackham captured the crew of a Dutch merchant ship.

One of the young English boys on board turned out to be a girl named Mary Read. The following year, Rackham, Anne and Mary were sentenced to death by hanging. But both women were spared the gallows because they were pregnant. Anne Bonny called Calico Jack a coward before he was hanged. We don't know what happened to her. Mary Read was kept in a Jamaican prison, where she died.

Dress like a pirate

Pirates needed to move quickly when they attacked other ships, so they wore loose, comfortable clothes. Many pirates also wore a hat or scarf to protect their head from the sun, and a sash or belt to hold weapons. Here are some ideas to help you dress like a swashbuckling pirate.

Pirate hat

1

Measure around your head with a tape measure. Draw a pirate-shaped hat onto some black card. The width across the bottom should be half the distance around your head, with a 1–2cm overlap.

Wear a neck scarf tied around your head

A pirate captain might wear a large hat to show his importance on board ship

Turn to pages 24–25 to find out how to make a pirate's dagger

Checked shirt

Loose, plain trousers

Striped t-shirt

Find out how to make a pirate flag on pages 16–17

Find out how to make a case for a map showing the location of buried treasure on pages 28–29

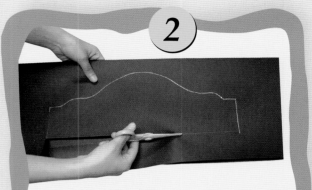

2

Cut out two pieces of card in the shape of your pirate hat. Glue the two pieces together using the 1–2cm overlap on the right and left edges.

3

Cut out a pirate symbol to decorate your hat

Cut out a strip of white paper or card to fit the top of your hat. Use pirate symbols, too. Glue them onto your hat.

Eye patch

If a pirate injured his eye in battle, he might need to wear an eye patch. You can easily cut an eye patch shape out of black card. Make a hole in either side and thread through a piece of black elastic.

Moustache

Cut a moustache shape out of thick black card, as shown. The small, rounded ends fit into your nostrils, to keep the moustache in place!

You will need

For the pirate hat:
- Tape measure
- Black card
- Pencil   • Scissors
- Glue
- White paper or thin card

For the eye patch and moustache:
- Card
- Scissors
- Black elastic

Corsairs and privateers

Some pirates were supported by their king, queen or government in times of war. They were called privateers and corsairs. They had permission to attack the merchant ships of other countries – but they usually had to share their plunder with their sponsor.

Clay pipe. Pirates smoked stolen tobacco

The Barbarossa brothers

In the 16th century, privateers along the Barbary coast of the Mediterranean were known as corsairs. Two of the most feared corsairs were the Turkish brothers Aruj and Kheir-ed-Din, whose beards gave them the nickname Barbarossa ('red-beard'). The Muslim brothers were the captains of large fleets that terrorized Christian ships and towns in search of treasure. Aruj was killed in 1518 by Spanish enemies but Kheir-ed-Din carried on fighting for the Sultan, the Turkish leader. He was made admiral-in-chief of the Sultan's great navy of 150 warships.

◀ Captain William Kidd was a famous 17th-century privateer. He sailed the Indian Ocean for the English king, William III, but was later hanged when the English government refused to support him.

Papal galley, a large ship with sails and oars

Papal and Spanish galleys usually had treasure on board

The Barbarossa ▶ brothers attacked quickly and without warning.

Hero or villain?

Sir Francis Drake (1543–96) made a famous voyage around the world in his ship the *Golden Hind*. Drake was an English sea captain and a privateer in the service of Queen Elizabeth I. During his voyage, he attacked ships and colonies belonging to the Spanish and Portuguese, in search of treasure.

Drake was an English hero – a great explorer and naval commander. But the Spanish thought differently. King Philip II of Spain demanded that Drake was punished for daring to steal Spanish treasure. Queen Elizabeth responded by congratulating Drake and making him a knight.

Aruj, the older Barbarossa brother

Mast. The galiot had one main sail, as well as oars

Crewmen were fearless and faithful

Kheir-ed-Din, whose name meant 'gift of God'

Light, fast ship called a galiot

Make a treasure chest

When pirates attacked a ship, they hoped to find a hold filled with treasure that would make them rich beyond their wildest dreams. In practice, they usually had to make do with robbing jewellery and cash. This project shows you how to make a treasure chest in which to keep your prized possessions!

Spanish treasure

Pirates hoped to rob a Spanish galleon laden with gold doubloons or silver dollars. Spanish silver dollars were first minted in 1497. Each coin was worth eight reals, and was often cut into four quarters or eight 'bits' to make small change. For this reason, the coins were sometimes called 'pieces of eight'.

▲ These 16th-century coins were recovered from a sunken Spanish ship.

Cut a piece of card the length of your shoebox and wide enough to curve over the top to make a dome-shaped lid.

You will need

- Rectangular shoebox
- Card
- Pencil
- Scissors
- Glue
- Brown and black paint
- Paintbrush
- Thick cardboard
- Paper fasteners

2

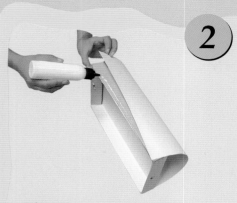

Glue the card onto the shoebox lid as shown. Draw around the curved sides of the lid onto another sheet of card.

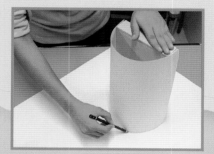

3

Cut out two curved pieces from the card, making them 1.5–2cm wider than your pencil mark. Cut flaps around the edges.

Fold over the flaps and glue them in place

Make a round lock and keyhole and glue it to the lid

4

Paint the lid and base of your treasure chest dark brown. Cut notches in a thick piece of card and use it to drag the paint into lines so it looks like wood.

Drag the paint with a cardboard 'comb' to get a wood grain effect

Glue cardboard 'straps' onto the lid and base. Push paper fasteners through the straps to look like studs

Pirate ships

The ships pirates used had to be fast enough to catch their victims and also to escape from chasing enemies. They had to be able to change course quickly and sail through creeks and shallow coves. Pirates preferred to get around in small, light ships.

Armed junk, a Chinese ship with sails and oars

▼ Chinese pirates attacked any European ships that dared to sail near their western Pacific coast.

Cloth or matting sails strengthened with bamboo

Prizes

Pirates called the ships they captured prizes. They often used these ships themselves. Successful pirates changed vessel frequently, making them even more difficult to recognize. A captured ship could be made more useful by adding guns and building up the ship's sides, to offer more protection.

 This modern schooner was built in the ▶ style of many pirate ships. It is sleek, with plenty of sails to make it fast.

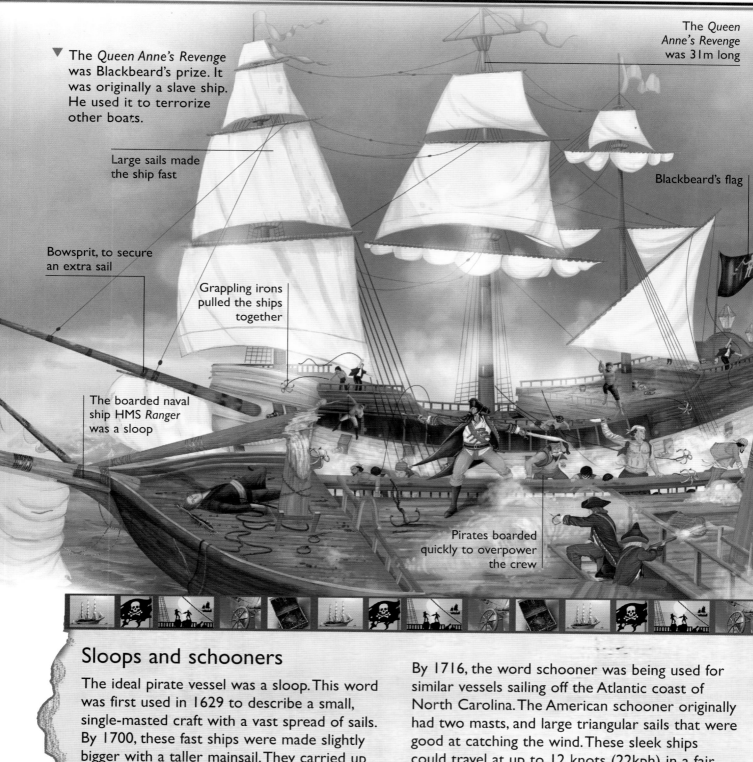

The *Queen Anne's Revenge* was Blackbeard's prize. It was originally a slave ship. He used it to terrorize other boats.

Large sails made the ship fast

The *Queen Anne's Revenge* was 31m long

Blackbeard's flag

Bowsprit, to secure an extra sail

Grappling irons pulled the ships together

The boarded naval ship HMS *Ranger* was a sloop

Pirates boarded quickly to overpower the crew

Sloops and schooners

The ideal pirate vessel was a sloop. This word was first used in 1629 to describe a small, single-masted craft with a vast spread of sails. By 1700, these fast ships were made slightly bigger with a taller mainsail. They carried up to 75 men and 14 cannons, but they could still sail in shallow water. Sloops were very popular with Caribbean buccaneers.

By 1716, the word schooner was being used for similar vessels sailing off the Atlantic coast of North Carolina. The American schooner originally had two masts, and large triangular sails that were good at catching the wind. These sleek ships could travel at up to 12 knots (22kph) in a fair wind. A schooner could carry a large crew, but the hold was small. Unfortunately, this meant there was less room for treasure!

Make a pirate flag

Many pirate ships flew a flag, known as a Jolly Roger. The name may have come from the English word 'rogue', which means a wandering vagabond, or from 'Old Roger' – a term for the devil. Plain red and black flags were the most common, but some flags were decorated with gruesome symbols, such as skulls, bones, swords or bleeding hearts. Look at some of these Jolly Roger designs, and then make your own pirate flag.

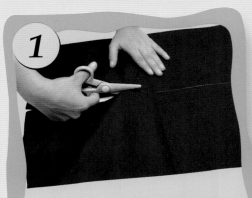

Cut a rectangle from the black fabric, measuring 90cm x 48cm. Turn over the two long edges and one short edge by 1–2cm and glue with fabric glue.

Glue the edges of the fabric so they will not fray

Pirate flag designs

Some pirate flags had symbols, such as skeletons, swords and hour-glasses. They were used to warn and scare sailors. The hour-glass, for example, showed the passing of time, before a grisly death!

Henry Avery's flag

Avery's flag showed a skull-and-crossbones. It has become a traditional pirate flag design.

Christopher Moody's flag

This flag had a winged hour-glass – to warn victims they only had so long to live.

Blackbeard's flag

Blackbeard's flag showed a devil-skeleton holding an hour-glass, and a bleeding heart.

2

Sketch a flag design onto paper. When you are happy with it, trace around it onto pieces of felt and cut out the shapes.

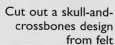

Cut out a skull-and-crossbones design from felt

3

Glue the design onto your flag. Then glue the edge of the flag to a stick or wooden broom pole using strong PVA glue.

The Jolly Roger was meant to scare the sailors of other ships into surrender. The most feared flag of all was a plain red flag which meant 'no quarter' – no prisoners would be taken and everyone on board would be killed.

Life on board

A pirate's life at sea was governed by a set of rules called ship's articles. This meant that everyone knew their job and the ship could run smoothly. Sometimes the rules were written down, and sailors had to swear an oath and sign the articles.

Running the ship

At sea, ordinary crewmen performed everyday tasks. Sails had to be hoisted, rigging needed checking and repairing, leaks needed mending and decks had to be scrubbed clean. Food was carefully stored below deck for journeys that could last for weeks at a time.

Everyone reported to the captain, but daily routine was left to the ship's second-in-command, the quartermaster. When a ship was captured, the quartermaster often took over the new vessel as captain. The captain and quartermaster were both elected by the crew.

Decks were scrubbed with water to keep them clean

The ship's carpenter was a busy man. There were always things to mend

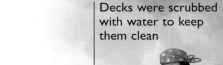

Piratical punishment

The ship's articles outlined crimes at sea. These included fighting, stealing, cheating at gambling games, cowardice in battle and bringing women aboard. Flogging was the common punishment for breaking rules. The offender was tied up and whipped on his bare back with the cruel cat-o'-nine-tails. The 'cat' was a whip made of nine knotted cords fastened to a handle.

If pirates were to be successful, it was important that the ship ran smoothly. Crewmen were encouraged to watch the flogging, to discourage them from breaking rules themselves.

Another painful punishment was keel-hauling. The victim was tied to a length of rope and thrown overboard. He was then dragged right under the ship and pulled up on the other side. The bottom of the ship would be covered in sharp barnacles, which meant the victim usually bled to death.

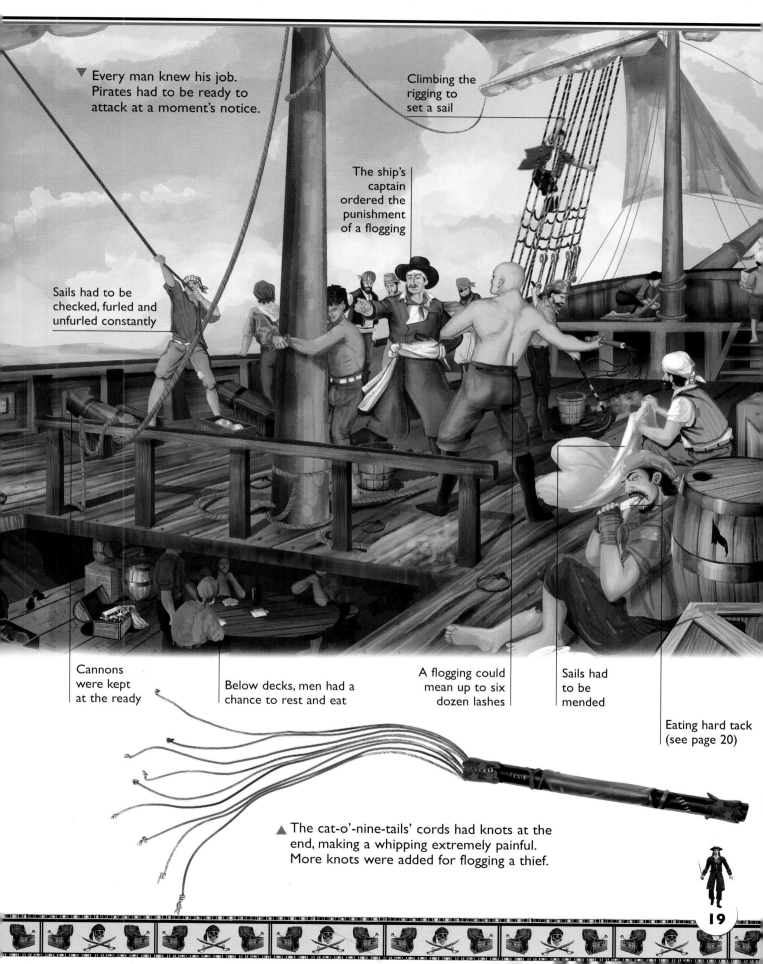

Every man knew his job. Pirates had to be ready to attack at a moment's notice.

Climbing the rigging to set a sail

The ship's captain ordered the punishment of a flogging

Sails had to be checked, furled and unfurled constantly

Cannons were kept at the ready

Below decks, men had a chance to rest and eat

A flogging could mean up to six dozen lashes

Sails had to be mended

Eating hard tack (see page 20)

The cat-o'-nine-tails' cords had knots at the end, making a whipping extremely painful. More knots were added for flogging a thief.

Make a pirate's fruit salad

Most pirates had a poor diet. They survived on biscuits or dried meat and when their stored water became stagnant, they drank beer or wine. A lack of vitamin C led to diseases, such as scurvy, which could cause teeth to fall out, sunken eyes and internal bleeding. When pirates reached shore they did everything they could to get their hands on fresh provisions. This project shows you how to make a fresh fruit salad, heaped in pineapple 'ships'.

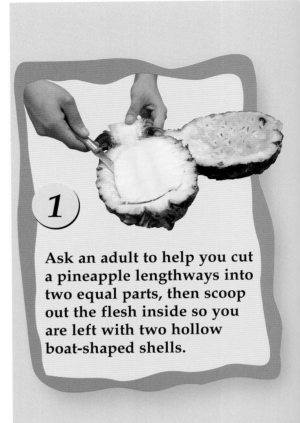

1

Ask an adult to help you cut a pineapple lengthways into two equal parts, then scoop out the flesh inside so you are left with two hollow boat-shaped shells.

Hard tack

Most ships were stocked with long-lasting biscuits made of coarse flour, salt and water. These biscuits were baked up to four times and were so tough that sailors called them 'hard tack' or 'molar breakers' (tack is a sailor's slang word for food). The biscuits often became infested with weevils. They were usually dunked in water, coffee or ale, or were used to thicken a stew of fish or dried meat.

Hard tack ▶ biscuits lasted a long time at sea.

Preventing scurvy

In 1753, James Lind, a Scottish surgeon in the British Royal Navy, published a book called *A Treatise of the Scurvy*. He described how the disease could be treated with citrus fruit, such as lemons and limes. The cause of scurvy was not known, but fruit helped!

2

With an adult's help, peel and chop different kinds of fruit, removing the seeds. Mix the fruit in a bowl, then pile it into the pineapple boats.

Colour a mini pirate flag onto a piece of paper

Sail made from white card

3

Cut a sail shape out of white card. Make slits in the top and bottom and slide though a wooden chopstick or skewer, to make a mast. Glue on a paper pirate flag, then push the mast into the ship.

You will need

Choose any fruits you like for your fruit salad. This salad uses:

- 1 pineapple
- 1 melon
- Coloured pen
- White card
- Wooden chopstick
- 1 papaya
- 2 mangoes
- Glue

Attack at sea

The element of surprise was all-important to pirates. On land, they would hang around ports to find out about ships with valuable cargoes. They would then sneak out to sea and follow their prey for days, waiting for the right moment to spring a surprise attack.

Grappling and boarding

When the wind was right and their target was within range, a pirate ship would hoist the Jolly Roger flag and close in fast. The gun crew would then spring into action, firing a few warning shots across the victim's bows.

Sometimes, they were able to take their prize without a fight. But if warnings were not enough, the ship's cannons would be fired in earnest. As the pirates came alongside the damaged ship, they would throw grappling irons into the rigging. The hooks would catch in the ropes, allowing the pirates to pull the ships closer together and leap aboard the enemy, for the fight to begin.

◀ Pirates attack a Spanish galleon in the Caribbean Sea. This kind of treasure ship was the greatest prize.

The small boarding craft tries to stay out of the galleon's sight and line of fire

Pirate weapons

During the 17th and 18th centuries, pirates used a sword called a cutlass, which had a short, broad blade. Longer swords were difficult to swing around when fighting at close quarters, and even got tangled in the rigging. Daggers, guns and pistols were also useful when capturing a ship. Pirates would carry a number of weapons so they could spring a surprise attack at any time.

Heavy musket slung over the shoulder

Pistol tucked into the belt

Cutlass held in a sheath

▼ Long-barrelled pistols were popular weapons. A spark lit gunpowder in the pistol's barrel, firing a lead ball.

This buccaneer ► guard is ready to use any of three kinds of weapons against thieves.

Muskets and pistols

Some pirates used muskets – these early guns had long barrels, which were fired from the shoulder. They could be used to kill enemy sailors before boarding. Once the pirates were on board the captured ship, however, muskets were too cumbersome. Most pirates chose to fight at close quarters with swords and daggers but until they were close enough, they also used their favourite boarding weapon – flintlock pistols. Pirates often carried several pistols stuffed in their belt. These guns had a short barrel. They fired a single lead ball and took time to reload, so pirates had to make every shot count!

Make a pirate's dagger

Daggers were a common weapon used by pirates. They were especially useful in small spaces below deck where there was no room to swing a sword. A dagger could also be concealed under clothing in a surprise attack. Pirates had to keep their wits about them, and a dagger was useful protection. This project shows you how to make your own pirate dagger.

Cut two tapered dagger blades from card, each around 30cm long.

Daggers

Almost every pirate wore a dagger. These knives usually had a sharp edge on both sides of the blade, and a sturdy handle to keep the pirate's hands away from the sharp metal. Daggers were thrust towards a victim at close range and were often used as the last means of self-defence in a fight. Pirates used daggers for other things, too. The blades were useful for cutting ropes and sails on board ship, or for slicing food to eat.

This 17th-century dagger ▶ shows a strong, sharp blade. The handles of daggers were often decorated.

You will need

- Corrugated card
- Scissors
- Strong PVA glue
- Silver foil
- White card
- Black tape
- Gold paint
- Glass 'jewels'

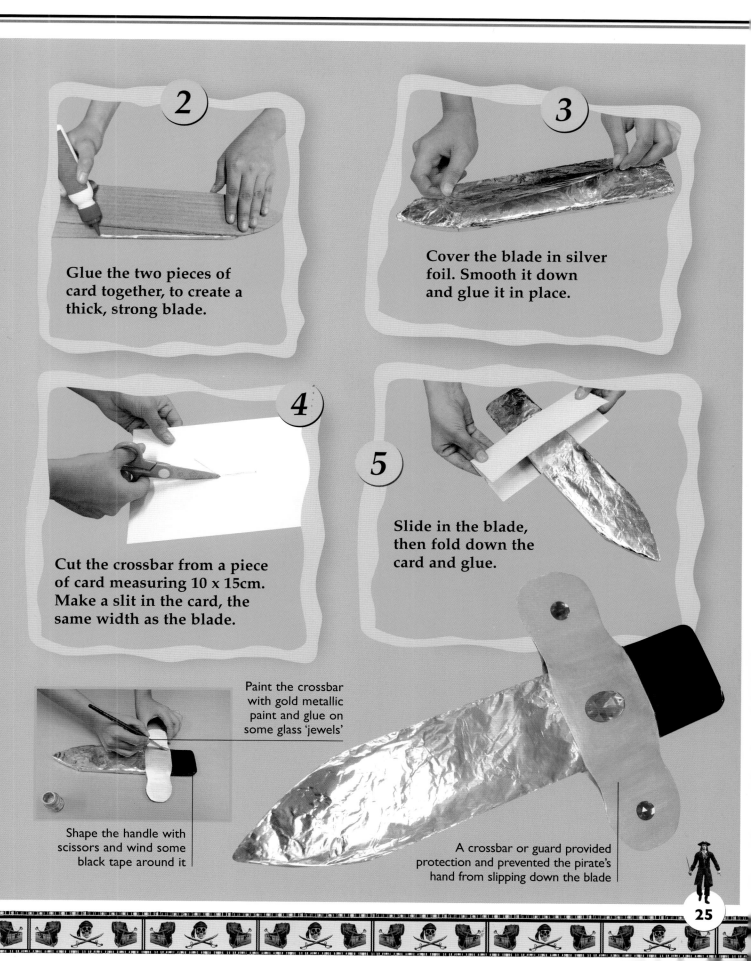

2 Glue the two pieces of card together, to create a thick, strong blade.

3 Cover the blade in silver foil. Smooth it down and glue it in place.

4 Cut the crossbar from a piece of card measuring 10 x 15cm. Make a slit in the card, the same width as the blade.

5 Slide in the blade, then fold down the card and glue.

Paint the crossbar with gold metallic paint and glue on some glass 'jewels'

Shape the handle with scissors and wind some black tape around it

A crossbar or guard provided protection and prevented the pirate's hand from slipping down the blade

Treasure!

In the 16th and 17th centuries, whole fleets of Spanish treasure ships sailed from the Americas to Europe. Their riches were easy to sell on land, making them a pirate's dream.

Fair shares

Gold and silver could be divided by weight, and coins were easy enough to share around. But jewels and other valuables had to be sold first. The treasure was then shared according to strict rules. Usually, the captain and quartermaster received two shares each. The ship's master, boatswain and gunner often got one and a half shares. The first mate and surgeon took one and a quarter shares. And ordinary crewmen had to settle for a single share each.

▲ Treasure chests were the most valuable goods carried at sea during the 16th and 17th centuries.

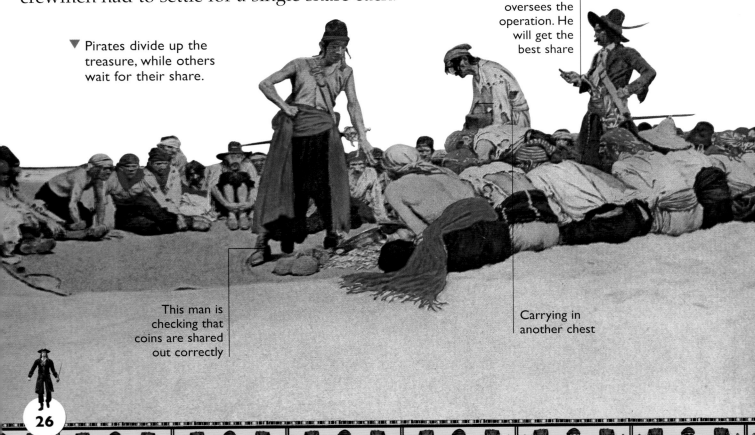

▼ Pirates divide up the treasure, while others wait for their share.

The captain oversees the operation. He will get the best share

This man is checking that coins are shared out correctly

Carrying in another chest

Buried treasure

There are all sorts of myths and legends about pirates' buried treasure. Unfortunately, most historians believe that the whole idea was probably made up. In fact, they say, very few pirates ever kept enough treasure to bury it. They generally sold and spent their ill-gotten gains as soon as they possibly could, before setting off on a new adventure.

Nevertheless, perhaps some treasure was buried and has simply never been found. Captain William Kidd, for example, is said to have hidden his loot on Gardiners Island, just off New York, in 1698. Some say most of it was found and handed to the authorities before Kidd was tried, found guilty of piracy and hanged. Stories like these encouraged most pirates to enjoy their spoils before they got caught!

◀ If Captain Kidd really did bury his treasure on an island, he certainly made sure it was well hidden.

Hiding places

When they were captured, some pirates tried to buy their way out of trouble by promising jailers untold riches. Stories claimed their vast wealth was hidden on a desert island, in a spot that only they knew. Sometimes, there were rumours of maps that identified the treasure's location. But more often than not, there was no treasure to be found at all!

Captain Kidd stands guard over his spoils

A crewman digs in the sand to bury the treasure

The chest is marked W.K. for William Kidd

Make a treasure map and case

There are lots of exciting stories about pirates and searches for lost, buried treasure. In *Treasure Island* by Robert Louis Stevenson, for example, a map of an island and a series of clues provide the means of discovering the pirates' hoard. In real life, however, pirates did not leave maps and clues. Even so, it's fun to make a map of your very own 'treasure island' – and a case to carry it in.

Treasure maps

Maps and sea charts were very valuable in the 16th and 17th centuries. They were the key to power and wealth in new territories, such as the Spanish Main. This was an area of South and Central America once ruled by Spain. It would later include the islands of the Caribbean – a popular playground for ambitious pirates!

This 16th-century map shows the Spanish Main. This area used to be full of pirates seeking their fortune.

Case

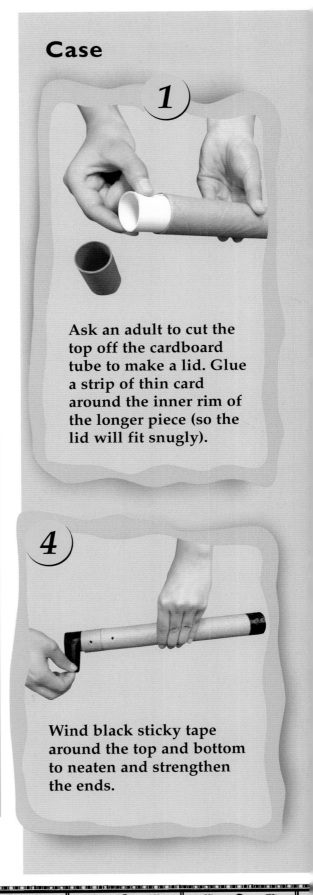

1 Ask an adult to cut the top off the cardboard tube to make a lid. Glue a strip of thin card around the inner rim of the longer piece (so the lid will fit snugly).

4 Wind black sticky tape around the top and bottom to neaten and strengthen the ends.

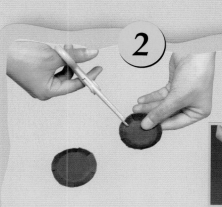

2

Cut two card circles, 2cm wider than the ends of the tube. Cut flaps around the circles and fold down.

Glue the circles onto the base of the tube and top of the lid

3

Ask an adult to make holes in the lid and at the top of the case with a single hole punch so you can thread through the leather cord.

Map

Take a sheet of white paper and make it look old – tear the edges, and stain it pale brown using a cool, used tea bag.

When the paper is dry, draw a map of your treasure island using coloured pens or pencils. You may want to add a dangerous reef, rocky coves, beaches, rivers and streams, palm trees, swamps and mountains. Add a compass rose – and don't forget to mark where the treasure is buried!

You will need

- Cardboard tube
- Scissors
- Glue
- Single hole punch
- Leather cord
- Thin card
- Black tape

5

Thread the leather cord through the lid and top of the case and knot securely. Roll up your map and keep it safe inside your map case!

Timeline

1399 English trader and pirate John Hawley captures 34 merchant ships off the coast of northern France.

1401 The famous Baltic Sea pirate Klaus Störtebeker, leader of the Victual Brothers, is captured and beheaded in Hamburg.

1518 The Barbarossa brothers gain control of Algiers.

1523 French corsair Jean Fleury raids three Spanish galleons full of Aztec treasure being sent from Mexico to Spain by Hernan Cortes.

1562 English privateer John Hawkins trades slaves between Africa and the West Indies.

1569 Dutch privateers known as 'sea beggars' attack Spanish ships.

1578 Francis Drake raids a number of Spanish ports in America.

1608 English nobleman Sir Francis Verney joins the Muslim Barbary corsairs and raids English merchant vessels.

1630 The Caribbean island of Tortuga becomes an infamous buccaneer base.

1660 Famous French buccaneer Jean David Nau (nicknamed L'Olonnais) makes a base for himself in Tortuga.

1674 Welsh pirate Henry Morgan is knighted by King Charles II and becomes deputy governor of Jamaica.

1697 Samuel Abraham, a pirate from Martinique in the Caribbean, takes over a French settlement in Madagascar and becomes known as King Samuel of Fort Dauphin.

1698 Captain William Kidd captures his most valuable prize, the Armenian ship *Quedagh Merchant*.

1700 The first known black flag with skull-and-crossbones is flown as a Jolly Roger.

1701 Captain Kidd is hanged in London for piracy.

1718 Edward Teach (otherwise known as Blackbeard) is killed.

1719 John Rackham (otherwise known as Calico Jack) plunders ships between Hispaniola and Bermuda.

1720 Female pirates Anne Bonny and Mary Read are tried in Jamaica.

1721 Famous Welsh pirate Bartholomew 'Barty' Roberts captures many ships off the coast of West Africa.

Glossary

Barbary coast The Mediterranean coast of North Africa.

Boatswain An officer in charge of a ship's sails and rigging.

Bowsprit A long pole sticking out from the bow (front) of a ship.

Buccaneer A pirate or privateer who raided Spanish ships and colonies in the Caribbean (West Indies).

Corsair A pirate or privateer of the Mediterranean region.

Cutlass A short sword with a curved blade.

Flintlock pistol An early gun in which a flint spark lit gunpowder.

Galiot A light, fast kind of galley.

Galleon A large, three-masted sailing ship used by the Spanish.

Galley A large ship powered by oars (and sometimes sails).

Grappling iron A set of hooks on a rope that could grab another ship.

Hard tack Ship's biscuits. Tack is slang for food.

Hold A space below deck for carrying cargo.

Jolly Roger A pirate flag.

Junk A Chinese ship.

Keel-hauling Dragging somebody under a boat as a severe punishment.

Mainsail The largest and most important sail on a ship.

Musket An early gun with a long barrel.

Pieces of eight Spanish silver coins.

Privateer Someone who is legally authorized to attack enemy ships.

Quartermaster A pirate officer, usually second in command to the captain.

Rigging System of ropes supporting a ship's masts and controlling the sails.

Schooner A small, fast, two- or three-masted sailing ship.

Scurvy A disease caused by a lack of Vitamin C.

Sloop A small, light, single-masted ship.

Spanish Main The sea off the coast of Central and South America and the Caribbean Islands, where Spanish treasure ships sailed for Europe.

Sponsor A person who supports and finances someone.

Index

Barbarossa brothers (Aruj and Kheir-ed-Din) 10, 11
Barbary coast 10
Blackbeard (Edward Teach) 4, 5, 15, 16
Bonny, Anne 7
buccaneers 4, 6, 7, 15

cannons 19, 22
Caribbean 4, 6, 15, 22, 28
cat-o'-nine-tails 18, 19
Charles II, King 6
Chinese pirates 14
corsairs 10
cutlass 5, 7, 23

dagger 8, 23, 24–25
doubloons 12
Drake, Francis 11

Elizabeth I, Queen 11

flags 8, 15, 16–17, 21, 22
  Blackbeard's 15, 16
  Christopher Moody's 16
  Henry Avery's 16
  Jolly Roger 16, 17, 22

Gardiners Island 27
grappling irons 15, 22

hard tack 19, 20

Kidd, William 10, 27

maps 4, 8, 27, 28–29
Mediterranean Sea 4, 10
Morgan, Henry 6

North Carolina 4, 15

Panama City 6

pistol 5, 23
privateers 10
punishment 18, 19

Queen Anne's Revenge 15

Rackham, Calico Jack 7
Read, Mary 7

schooner 15
scurvy 20
skull-and-crossbones 8, 16, 17
sloop 15
Spanish Main 4, 28
sword 7, 24

treasure 4, 5, 6, 10–11, 12–13, 22, 26–27, 28, 29

William III, King 10

Webfinder

http://www.nmm.ac.uk/server/show/conWebDoc.159
An introduction to pirates from the National Maritime Museum.

http://www.piratesinfo.com
Piratical facts and biographies.

http://www.thepiratesrealm.com
Lots of information about famous pirates, ships and flags.

http://www.nationalgeographic.com/pirates
National Geographic's 'High Seas Adventure'.